The AMERICAN CENTURY SERIES

LAWRENCE
POLICE DEPARTMENT
HEROES WEAR BLUE

The American Century Series

Lawrence
Police Department

Heroes Wear Blue

Ronald J. DeSantis

ARCADIA

Published by Arcadia Publishing,
an imprint of Tempus Publishing, Inc.
2 Cumberland Street
Charleston, SC 29401

Printed in Great Britain.

Library of Congress Catalog Card Number: 99-62618

For all general information contact Arcadia Publishing at:
Telephone 843-853-2070
Fax 843-853-0044
E-Mail edit@arcadiaimages.com

For customer service and orders:
Toll-Free 1-888-313-BOOK

Visit us on the internet at http://www.arcadiaimages.com

*I would like to dedicate this work to the men and women
of the City of Lawrence Police Department.
No finer law enforcement agency exists anywhere,
who do what they do and with what they have to work with.
They are the real writers of this work;
without their proud history there would be no book.*

—Ronald J. DeSantis
1999

About the Author: Ronald J. DeSantis is a Vietnam Veteran, who continues serving his country as a Peace Officer with the Lawrence Police Department, where he has entered his 27th year. An author and historian, Officer DeSantis holds the official title of "Lawrence Police Department Historian in Residence" and is also a published short story writer and internationally published poet.

CONTENTS

ACKNOWLEDGMENTS

I would like to thank all of those who have submitted photographs and information to this work. When known, the photographer or sources are named. Most of the photographs were not marked or were merely copies of originals without the source of their origins.

I thank following for the use of photographs:

The Lawrence Eagle Tribune
Mark E. Vogler, News Photographer
Gillian Mahon, Professional Photographer
Micheline (Mahon) Cacciatore, Professional Photographer
Lt. Stanley Bachta, photographer, Lawrence Police Department
William Wolfindale, Lawrence Police Department
The Lawrence Police Relief Association
The Lawrence Public Library

All the profits from the sale of this book have been donated by the author to the Lawrence Police Relief Association. The Lawrence Police Relief Association is a benevolent, non-profit association established by the Lawrence Police on April 6, 1889.

Advance Apology

I would like to apologize in advance for the omission, mislabeling, or misspelling of anyone's name. The handling of thousands of names leaves little doubt as to this happening. My sincerest apologies.

INTRODUCTION

This pictorial history, *Lawrence Police Department: Heroes Wear Blue*, records a proud account of service to the Lawrence community from its inception in 1847 up to the present day, 1999, two years past its 150-year anniversary. It includes photographs from the Civil War era to the present day. The history is not meant to be a book of funny anecdotes or stories done in police lingo. It is meant only to be a necessarily limited pictorial history of the police department, its men, its equipment, and its heroes.

Although the physical locations, uniforms, and equipment have changed, the officers have not in spirit. They still raise families, juggle finances, laugh and tease with gallows humor, and, yes, even cry, just as they have for the last 152 years. They are human, just like you and me, and are subject to the same strengths and weaknesses. They are looked upon as strong and capable, as someone to protect us, who will react with calm and courage when the rest of us cannot. These fathers, mothers, sisters, brothers, neighbors, and friends are the only thing, a long thin blue line, that stands between the criminals in our society and you, our families.

From the bottom of my heart I wish I could thank each and every one of them personally for a job well done. The City of Lawrence Police Department is one of the finest in the world and I am proud to be a member.

—Ronald. J. DeSantis

Heroes Wear Blue

What kind of persons
would leave their homes
on cold and stormy nights?
Rushing to chase bad guys,
breaking up barroom fights.
They patrol the streets of America
to tame this troubled land.
Hoping in their hearts
they never have to draw
their weapons so close at hand.
Lost dogs, lost kids
shoplifters at the malls.
Vagrants, drunks and thieves,
drug addicts in the halls.
Eight short hours, a lifetime
for the police who work the streets.
Donut shops and fast foods,
broken bodies under sheets.
But when their watch is over
they slowly drift back home.
Life and death held in their hands
they find themselves alone.
Who are these men and women,
these heroes who wear blue?
They're fathers, wives, brothers
and they are known to me and you.

—Ronald J. DeSantis, 1997

One

HISTORY

AND LEADERSHIP

DAY SHIFT, OUTSIDE THE LAWRENCE POLICE DEPARTMENT ON THE CORNER OF LAWRENCE STREET AND COMMON STREET, 1947. The police officers, shown here from left to right, are as follows: (front row) Chief Martin O'Sullivan, Capt. Daniel Hart, Capt. Francis Traynor, Police Commissioner Louis Scanlon, Lieutenant Pendergast, Sgt. Joseph Jordan, and Officer George Connors; (second row) Timothy O'Leary, Jack O'Neil, Jerry Potvin, Joseph Fallon, Frank Foley, and Charles Haffner; (third row) Philip Larco, William Barrett, Charles Collins, Leonard Dunn, George Roche, and Joseph Naughton; (fourth row) Oscar Hilbert, Walter Sliva, Francis Incropera Jr., and Michael Lyons; (fifth row) Daniel Papa, Daniel Murphy, William Lees, and Charles Kennan; (sixth row) Jerry Regan, Walter Costello, Frank Wycislak, Fred Gilmartin, and Daniel Shine.

THE OLDEST-KNOWN PHOTOGRAPH OF A LAWRENCE POLICE OFFICER IN UNIFORM. Both his badge and this *c.* 1880 photograph were purchased by the author at an antique shop in Gettysburg, Pennsylvania.

MOULTON BATCHELDER ON THE LEFT. Moulton served the City of Lawrence in the Civil War as an officer in the 6th Massachusetts Company K. He served as city marshall from 1875 to 1877, then again from 1878 to 1881. This photograph was taken at Hall Studio at 142 Essex Street in 1864. (Courtesy of U.S. Military History Institute.)

CHASE PHILBRICK. A lieutenant colonel in the Mass 15th Volunteers, Chase Philbrick was wounded at the Battle of Fredericksburg. He served as chief of the Lawrence Police Department from August 8, 1864, to 1870, and then again from 1871 to 1873. He left to become one of the first Massachusetts state detectives, forerunners of our modern state police detectives. (Courtesy of U.S. Military History Institute.)

OFFICER TIMOTHY KELLEHER IN A LAWRENCE POLICE DEPARTMENT UNIFORM. Officer Kelleher died in the late 1890s. These Bobbie-style hats were worn up until about 1915.

11

OFFICER WILLIAM AHEARN, c. 1915.
Officer Ahearn was one of the first police officers in the city to carry a business card to hand out to victims of crimes.

LAWRENCE CITY HALL IN THE 1870s. This building, complete with Civil War cannon balls on the exterior, was once the site of the first city lockup. The prisoners were kept in wooden cells built into the archways of the basement. (Used with permission of the Lawrence Public Library.)

THE COMBINATION
LAWRENCE POLICE
STATION AND
COURTHOUSE IN THE
LATE 1890S. The red
brick, Mansard-roofed,
three-story building
stood on the corner of
Lawrence Street and
Common Street until
1914, when it was
torn down and
replaced.
(Stereoscopic view,
taken by A.B. Hamor,
Lawrence,
Massachusetts.)

A POSTCARD OF THE LAWRENCE POLICE DEPARTMENT AND COURTHOUSE. This structure was
built in 1914 to replace an older wooden one with a Mansard roof. It stood at the corner of
Lawrence Street and Common Street until 1965, when it was torn down and a new one was
built on the present site of 90 Lowell Street. (Postcard published by E.E. Smith.)

THE CYCLONE OF 1890. This photograph depicts the aftermath of a cyclone that touched down in South Lawrence on July 26, 1890. You can clearly see a Lawrence police officer, wearing the uniform of the day. (Used with permission of the Lawrence Public Library.)

MORE DAMAGE FROM THE CYCLONE OF 1890. It struck without warning on a warm day in July and caught Lawrencians totally off guard. A police officer guarding the scene is in the foreground. (Used with permission of the Lawrence Public Library.)

14

THE SUMMER OF 1890. The cyclone, which left the above damage, left 6 Lawrence residents dead and 95 injured. A family can be seen standing in the rubble of what once was their home. Lawrence police officers stood guard against looting. (Used with permission of the Lawrence Public Library.)

DENNIS F. MURPHY, 1924. His son, Dennis M. Murphy, is a Lawrence police officer today.

A FINE-LOOKING GROUP OF LAWRENCE POLICE DETECTIVES IN THE EARLY 1900s. Shown here are, from left to right, Capt. Daniel Kiley (standing), Joseph Sullivan, Capt. Martin O'Sullivan, unidentified, and Detective Lt. Fred Lannen.

A 1947 GROUP PHOTOGRAPH. Shown outside the old police station on Common Street, from left to right, are as follows: (front row) Officer Timothy Nolan, Deputy Chief Arthur Reily, and Officer Joseph Hayes; (back row) Officer Jerry Donovon and Inspector Tad Sullivan.

16

THE GOD AND COUNTRY PARADE, SEPTEMBER 12, 1962. This parade celebrated the 50th anniversary of the Lawrence Strike of 1912, which is better known as The Bread and Roses Strike. The parade started on Broadway and Whitman Streets. Participants marched south to Essex Street, east on Essex Street to Jackson Street, north on Jackson Street to Haverhill Street, and west on Haverhill Street to the reviewing stand in front of the Oliver School. Shown here, from left to right, are as follows: (first row) Chief Charles F. Hart; (second row) Charles Burzlaff, Edward A. Lawlor, Joseph Golden, Fred J. Childs, and Clayton M. Dunn; (third row) Daniel J. Lannon, Alfred Duemling, John E. Farrington, Martin V. Hanley, and George W. Andrews; (fourth row) Frank B. Concemi and Martin J. Blake; (fifth row) Julius V. Volungus, Gilbert H. Hulme, Walter J. Sliva, and Jeremiah S. Donovon.

STANDING THE LAST WATCH IN AUGUST 1965. Officer Jerry Houlihan was the last officer on watch at the old police station at Lawrence Street and Common Street. The next day, communications were switched over to the new police station.

THE DEDICATION OF THE NEW POLICE STATION AT 90 LOWELL STREET. A new police flag was acquired for a new police station. Shown here, from left to right, are Ald. of Public Safety Vincent Foley, Chief Charles F. Hart, and Patrolman Francis Landers.

THE NEW POLICE STATION AT 90 LOWELL STREET.

THE DEDICATION OF THE NEW POLICE STATION AT 90 LOWELL STREET, AUGUST 1965.
Shown here, from left to right, are as follows: (sitting) Ald. of Public Safety Vincent P. Foley, Chief Charles F. Hart, unidentified, and Mayor John J. Buckley; (standing) Judge Paul Perocchi, Judge Darcey, Attorney Batel, Father Carney, District Attorney John J. Burke, unidentified, and Officer Francis Landers.

MOULTON BATCHELDER. Batchelder served as the Lawrence City Marshall from 1875 to 1877, then again from 1878 to 1881. (Photograph courtesy of U.S. Military History Institute.)

JAMES T. O'SULLIVAN. O'Sullivan was the Lawrence City Marshal from 1877 to 1878, from 1882 to 1885, from 1886 to 1888, from 1900 to 1906, and again from 1911 to 1912.

CHARLES R. VOSE, CITY MARSHAL FROM 1932 UNTIL 1945.

MARTIN V. O'SULLIVAN.
O'Sullivan served Lawrence as
chief of police from 1945 to 1949.

**CHIEF OF POLICE FRANCIS J.
TRAYNOR.** Traynor served as
chief from 1950 until 1952.

LAWRENCE POLICE DEPARTMENT CHIEF OF POLICE DANIEL P. KILEY. Kiley served as chief from 1952 to 1958.

CHARLES F. HART, CHIEF OF THE LAWRENCE POLICE DEPARTMENT FROM 1958 TO 1978. Hart served as chief in both the Lawrence and Common Streets station and the new station at 90 Lawrence Street.

**PATRICK SCHIAVONE, LAWRENCE
CHIEF OF POLICE FROM 1980 TO 1983.**
Patrick's brother Terrence also became a
police officer and later served as the
Lawrence Director of Public Safety. His
father, Carl Schiavone, was a captain of
detectives in Lawrence.

JOSEPH TYLUS, LAWRENCE POLICE
CHIEF FROM 1983 TO 1989.

THOMAS NASTASIA. Capt. Thomas Nastasia served from 1987 to 1989 as acting chief.

JOSEPH ST. GERMAIN. Lt. Joseph St. Germain served as acting chief from 1993 to 1995.

ALLAN COLE. Cole served as chief from 1989 to 1993.

ROBERT E. HAYDEN JR., CHIEF FROM 1995 TO 1997. Hayden came to Lawrence from the Boston Police Department.

JOHN J. ROMERO, LAWRENCE POLICE CHIEF FROM 1999 TO PRESENT. Romero came from New York City, where he served as precinct chief with the 34th Precinct. He replaced Ronald J. Guilmette, who served from 1997 to 1999.

Two

TOOLS OF THE TRADE

JERIMIAH DONOVON, ON A 1947 HARLEY DAVIDSON MOTORCYCLE IN FRONT OF THE STATION HOUSE AT COMMON STREET AND LAWRENCE STREET.

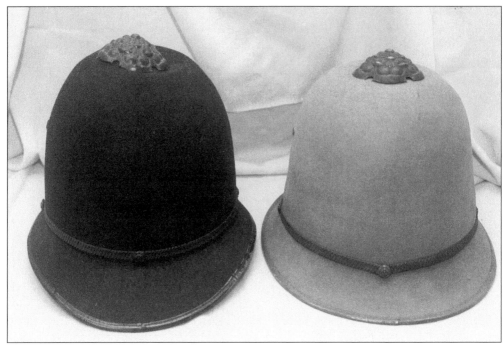

HIGH HATS. These two hats, designed after the English Bobbie hats, were standard issue and were used by the Lawrence Police Department from 1847 to about 1915. The black one on the left was used for winter wear; the one on the right is brown and was used for summer wear. They belonged retired Lt. Inspector Fred Lannen.

STANDARD-ISSUE BELT. This black leather belt with its two-piece buckle was standard issue from the 1800s to about 1915. It was worn around the waist of a heavy, woolen, double-breasted, calf-length coat.

CRIMINAL JEWELRY. Handcuffs, like those seen in the upper left, were used by Lawrence police officers in the late 1800s. The pair in the upper right was used in the early 1900s; they belong to retired Officer Michael J. Carelli. He used this pair from 1972 until his retirement in 1995. The pair on the lower left is the type still used today.

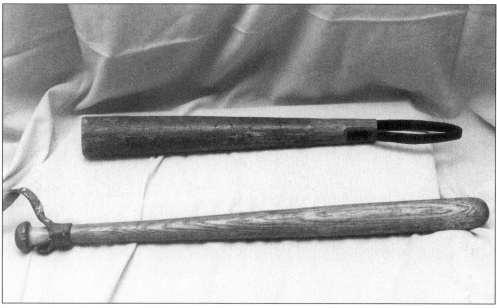

CRUDE, BUT EFFECTIVE. These two billy clubs were actually carried by Lawrence police officers. The one on top was homemade; it looks like a leg of furniture. Retired Police Chief Charles Vose carried it. The one on the bottom is approximately 2 feet long.

AN 1890s BADGE. This badge was loaned by retired Police Lt. Francis Incropera and his wife, Dorothy. The badge was worn by Mrs. Incropera's grandfather, Lt. James F. McMahon. It sits in a leather case that advertises for an insurance company on Amesbury Street in Lawrence.

AN 1960s PHOTOGRAPH. It's off to pick up prisoners in the new patrol wagon. The driver, William Pedrick, talks to Officer Joseph St. Germain.

A Booking Room Camera. This camera was used from the 1950s until the 1980s, when it was replaced by computer imaging. A prisoner would hold up a metal piece with the arrest number for the year and the date of the arrest. Film was then placed into the camera and two photographs were taken. One photo was taken straight on and the other was a profile.

The History of the Lawrence Police Badge. The oldest badge, from the 1800s, is on the top left; the newest, from 1999, is on the bottom right.

FIREARMS USED BY THE LAWRENCE POLICE DEPARTMENT THROUGH THE YEARS. In the center bottom is a nickel-plated Hopkins & Allen Arms Co. .32-cal. short break top revolver model Safety Police. On the left side bottom is a detective issue six-shot Smith and Wesson 2-inch snub nose round butt k-frame revolver. To the upper left is a colt .38 Caliber Police Positive revolver. On the lower right is a Smith and Wesson .38 special revolver model #10 k frame. Above center is a .9mm Sig Sauer P226 15-shot semi-automatic pistol. On the top right is a Smith and Wesson Model #66 stainless steel .357 cal. k-frame revolver.

TWO MACHINE GUNS AND A PISTOL. The top weapon is a Thompson Sub-Machine Gun, which were widely used up to and including the 1960s. Today they are highly prized collectables on the gun market. They fired .45 cal. bullets on full automatic and had a 75-round drum magazine. Second down is a Heckler & Kotch .9mm sub-machine gun. It is a model MP-5 SD and is now used in Lawrence. Last is a .9mm semi-automatic pistol made by Sig-Sauer.

DUAL FORCE. Some Lawrence police officers wore two badges; they were also sworn into the Essex County Sheriff's Department, which increased their legal jurisdiction to include the entire county. Shown here, from left to right, are Officer Michael J. Carelli, Sgt. Samuel Coco (rear), Lt. Francis Incropera III, and Officer Ronald J. DeSantis.

TEST PILOT FOR THE LAWRENCE POLICE DEPARTMENT. Officer Willey Arlequeew was a test officer for a company trying to market an officer's safety helmet. It was made with a bright-blue flashing light on top so that the traffic officer could be seen from a distance. It did not sell.

MOUNTED OFFICER JOHN CASEY AS A YOUNG OFFICER IN THE 1920s. Casey would soon work his way up the ranks and retire as a captain from the Lawrence Police Department.

INTRODUCING TWO NEW FOUR-LEGGED MEMBERS TO THE DEPARTMENT. Seen standing, from left to right, are as follows: (front row) an unidentified Boston police mounted training officer, Lt. Walter Soriano, Mayor Kevin Sullivan, and Chief of Police Joseph S. Tylus; (rear) Mounted Officer Charles M. Midolo (sitting atop Diamond) and Mounted Officer Michael Misserville (on Pepsi).

Motorcycles

In 1995, under the direct supervision of Capt. David Kelley, the motorcycles were brought back after many years' absence. This was done under the orders of Chief Robert E. Hayden Jr. He had come from Boston, where he had seen their effectiveness first-hand. The team started with 6 motorcycles and has since been increased to 12. The teams work days and the early night shift. Lieutenant Pierce is the line supervisor for the team that rides from March to December. Harley Davidson is their only choice in motorcycles.

MOTORCYCLES LINED-UP OUTSIDE THE STATION HOUSE ON THE CORNER OF LAWRENCE STREET AND COMMON STREET IN 1931. The motor officers in the photograph are unidentified as they line up to show off some now classic Harley Davidson motorcycles.

MOTOR OFFICERS IN 1938. Shown here are Officer Daniel A. Lyons (left) and William Ludwig.

MOTOR OFFICER DANIEL A. LYONS OUTSIDE THE LAWRENCE POLICE STATION IN THE 1930S. Lyons is wearing the classic motor officer's uniform of the day.

SHOWING OFF STATE-OF-THE-ART EQUIPMENT IN CRIME FIGHTING IN THE 1950S. Shown here on the Harley Davidson motorcycles, from left to right, are Daniel J. Lannon (who would retire as a detective), Joseph Moynihan, Jerome Lucchesi, and Sgt. Arthur Morris. Inside the police cruiser is Teddy Bardwell.

NEW EQUIPMENT BEING INTRODUCED. Four new three-wheeled motorcycles, servi cars, were added to the traffic patrol force. Shown here, from left to right, are Ald. of Public Safety Vincent P. Foley, Officer William Pedrick, Officer Willy Arlequeew, Police Chief Charles F. Hart, Deputy Chief Arthur Riley, Daniel Kiley, and Officer James Castles.

MOTORCYCLE OFFICERS IN THE 1960S. Shown here, from left to right, are Steven Sciuto, who would attain the rank of captain; Alfred Duemling, who would later reach the rank of sergeant and transfer to the Massachusetts State Police; Jerry Lucchesi; John McGowen; and Joseph Fitzpatrick, who would reach the rank of captain and retire as chief of the detective division.

MOTOR OFFICER ALFRED DUEMLING IN THE 1960S, COMPLETE WITH THE LATEST IN SAFETY HEADGEAR. Officer Duemling would rise to the rank of sergeant in the Lawrence Police Department and then transfer to the Massachusetts State Police as a lieutenant detective.

MOTORCYCLE OFFICERS OFFICER JOSEPH ST. GERMAIN (LEFT) AND HIS PARTNER, OFFICER WILLIAM PEDRICK, IN 1964.

TRAFFIC OFFICER WILLIAM BARRY. Officer Barry smiles for the camera in this 1960s photograph. As far as safety gear goes, we have come a long way.

STEVEN SCIUTO. Motor Patrol Officer Sciuto rose to the rank of captain within the Lawrence Police Department. He was in charge of the traffic division.

TRAFFIC PATROL OFFICER JOSEPH PERUSE, 1962.

MOTORCYCLE OFFICER THOMAS CARROLL IN THE 1960s, ON HIS 3-WHEEL HARLEY DAVIDSON SERVI CAR. This vehicle was used for traffic control and enforcement. The compartment was used for storage.

HAPPY SAINT PATRICK'S DAY. Motorcycle Officer James Kiley pauses during the Saint Patrick's Day parade to pose with, on his left, Monsignor Burke from Saint Patrick's Church, and on his right, the Reverend Harold Lawson.

PARADE DUTY. Shown here, from left to right, are Motor Officer James Castles, who would later rise to the rank of lieutenant; Sam Nitto; William Walsh; and Capt. Thomas Nastasia, who would make the rank of captain and serve as the Lawrence Police Department's acting chief.

JOHN CAVERETTA. Motor Officer Caveretta poses for a photograph in the 1960s on Jackson Street in front of the Masonic Temple.

MOTORCYCLES IN 1997. This photograph was taken on July 9, 1997, in front of the police station at 90 Lowell Street. Shown here, from left to right, are Sgt. James S. Crocker, Officer Joseph Padellaro, Officer Alan Andrews, Officer Jose Flores Jr., Officer Michael McCarthy, Lt. Dennis Pierce, Officer Kevin Callahan, Officer Thomas Murphy, Capt. David Kelley, Officer James Fitzpatrick, Officer Roy Vasque, and Officer Stephen Scheffen.

PROUD TO BE A MEMBER. Motor Officer Michael McCarthy proudly displays his new motorcycle. It was earned after many rigorous hours of motorcycle training.

A 1950s Photograph Taken on Lawrence Street. Shown here, from left to right, are Teddy Bardwell (standing); Arthur Morris (driving the cruiser), who would later rise to the rank of sergeant; Officer Frank Concemi (standing), who would retire as sergeant; and Lt. Francis Incropera Jr., giving the orders. In the rear of the cruiser is an unidentified officer.

Heavy with Brass. Shown here are, from left to right, Deputy Chief Arthur Riley; Lt. Vincent P. Foley, who would later become director of public safety; Capt. Andrew Griffin; and Sgt. Joseph O'Connor.

44

Three

RECREATION
AND SOCIAL LIFE

A MEMORIAL DAY PARADE IN 1954. The Lawrence Police Honor Guard marches in a parade west on Haverhill Street at the intersection with Lawrence Street. Shown here, from left to right, are Officer Daniel J. Lannon, Officer Alex Lawn, Officer Francis Landers, and Officer Joseph Moynahan. Parades, historically, have been an important part of the police department's special functions. To the general public it showed unity, strength, and camaraderie within the police troops. It gave the public a sense of well-being to see their police officers on review. To the officers, it was a social activity. It gave them the chance to see their fellow officers from other shifts. It was a time when families came together, proudly, to see their husbands and wives on parade.

PROUD TO BE MARCHING. Officers wear dress uniforms with white gloves and white parade batons.

MARCHING EAST ON HAVERHILL STREET AT THE INTERSECTION WITH EAST HAVERHILL STREET. The third officer from the left is Nicholas Trianello; the fifth from the left is Officer Carl Shiavone. Officer Schiavone rose to the rank of captain and retired as captain of detectives.

MARCHING NORTH ON CROSS STREET. Lawrence officers march for a May parade. Saint Francis School is on the right of the photograph; the steeple of Saint Mary's Church can be seen in the background.

A 1950S PARADE INSPECTION OUTSIDE OF THE LAWRENCE AND COMMON STREETS POLICE STATION. Officers line up outside the Common Street entrance. Shown here, from left to right, are Chief Martin O'Sullivan; Officer Philip DiAdimo, who would later attain the rank of captain and become the Lawrence Commissioner of Public Safety; Officer John Morrison; Officer Martin Hanley; Officer Clement Bennert; Officer James Golden, who would later become a sergeant; Officer Alfred Donovan, who would reach the rank of captain, become the public safety commissioner for Lawrence, and fill in as the acting chief; Officer John Concannon; Officer Vincent P. Foley, who would reach the rank of lieutenant and become the Lawrence Director of Public Safety; and Deputy Chief Arthur Reilly.

Honor Guard at Parade Rest in the North Common. Shown here, from left to right, are Officer Daniel J. Lannon, Officer John Spanks, Officer Sam Incropera, and Officer Domonic Armano, who, after retirement, ran successfully and served as a Lawrence city councilor.

Charles Vose, Leading the Parade, c. early 1940s. Chief Vose led the parade until his retirement in 1945. Vose joined the Lawrence Police Department in the late 1800s and rose through the ranks to become its chief. The parade, most likely a May procession for Saint Mary's Grammar School in the background, marches west on Haverhill Street near the intersection of Hampshire Street.

A PARADE GROUP, PHOTOGRAPHED *c.* 1950S. The sergeant leading this parade group is Francis Incropera Jr., who would later become and retire as a lieutenant. Shown here, from left to right, are Officer Salvatore J. Rapisardi, who would attain the rank of lieutenant; William Pedrick; Officer Pat Vivenzio; unidentified; Officer Philip Angelone, who would make sergeant; Charles Vivenzio; and Nicholas Trionello.

A MILITARY/POLICE FUNERAL FOR OFFICER JAMES F. TATTAN, AUGUST 4, 1941. Officer Tattan was on leave from the Lawrence Police Department to serve as a lieutenant in the U.S. Army. He was stationed at Fort Sill, Oklahoma, when he became ill and died of a cerebral hemorrhage at the base hospital on July 26, 1941. His flag-draped coffin is seen here atop a gun carriage arriving in front of Saint Mary's Church for his funeral mass as Lawrence police officers pass into the church.

THE CHIEF OF POLICE LEADING THE WAY. On the left and leading the troops in the early 1940s is Chief of Police Charles Vose.

A PARADE IN THE LATE 1940S OR EARLY 1950S. Officers marched in parade dress with high-necked woolen coats, white parade batons, and white gloves.

LAWRENCE'S FINEST, MARCHING WEST ON HAVERHILL STREET AND APPROACHING THE INTERSECTION OF HAMPSHIRE STREET, IN THE LATE 1950S. This fine group is led by Chief of Police Daniel P. Kiley. Fourth from the left is Officer Frank Concemi and fifth is Officer Alfred Donovan.

MARCHING SOUTH ON SOUTH BROADWAY IN THE EARLY 1960S. Chief Hart, just behind the color guard, proudly leads his men. Behind and to his right, Congressman William X. Wall is wearing the straw hat. Officer Alex Lawn, with the rifle, and Officer Jerimiah Donovon, carrying the Lawrence Police Department flag, are the only members of the color guard that are identifiable.

A PARADE IN THE EARLY 1960S. This parade is moving south on Broadway, just passing Arlington Street. Marching in the front left of the honor guard is Officer Daniel J. Lannon; Officer Francis Landers, carrying the Massachusetts State Flag, would later reach the rank of sergeant; and Chief Daniel P. Kiley leads the parade. To the left in the line of officers marching is William Barry; Officer William McGuigan marches next to him.

MARCHING EAST ON HAVERHILL STREET ON THE NORTH SIDE OF SAINT MARY'S CHURCH. The color guard shown here are, from left to right, Officer Joseph Moynahan; Sgt. Clifford Brennan, who would later make lieutenant; Officer Jerimiah Donovon; and Officer John (Taffy) McCann. In the rear and leading the men is Officer Francis Landers.

COLOR GUARD IN THE LATE 1960s. Shown here, from left to right, are Sgt. Thomas Nastasia, Officer Willy Arlequeew, Officer Paul Sutton, and Sgt. Steven Sciuto. Senator William X. Wall is up on the stage in the rear, wearing a soft hat. Chief Charles F. Hart sits in the front, center stage.

A MAY PROCESSION IN FRONT OF THE HOLY ROSARY SCHOOL ON GARDEN STREET, 1948. The men are being lead by Capt. Arthur J. Reiley, who later would become deputy chief. Shown here, from left to right, are an unidentified officer, Officer Gino Puglisi, Officer Philip C. DiAdamo, Officer Francis J. Incropera Jr., Officer Carl R. Schiavone, Officer Nicholas A. Trianello, Officer Pasquale J. Vivenzio, and Officer Philip Larco.

A MAY PROCESSION IN THE LATE 1950s BEING LED BY CHIEF DANIEL P. KILEY. These officers seem to be paying more attention to who is in step than to what is going on around them.

A RARE VIEW LOOKING WEST DOWN ESSEX STREET IN THE 1960s. The police group is approaching Lawrence Street during the 100th Anniversary of Lawrence Parade. It's great to see some of the old stores that once lined Essex Street.

A PARADE PASSING IN FRONT OF THE POLICE STATION ON LAWRENCE STREET. This parade is going south toward Essex Street. The color guard, from left to right, are John (Taffy) McCann, Sgt. Clifford Brennan, Officer Jerimiah Donovon, and Officer Alfred Duemling. Chief Hart, directly behind, leads his men.

THE LAWRENCE POLICE DEPARTMENT MARCHING NORTH ON SOUTH BROADWAY IN THE 1920S. This photograph was taken in front of Saint Patrick's Church at the intersection of South Broadway and Salem Street. The only officer identified is Officer Theadore (Tad) Sullivan, on the far left.

JUNE 6, 1960. The Lawrence Police Department marches north on Jackson Street at Garden Street. Just behind the color guard, the parade is being lead by Chief Charles F. Hart and Director of Public Safety Vincent P. Foley. To Foley's right is Officer Francis Landers. Just behind the departments' officers and in front of the main body of officers, we can see a contingent of Massachusetts State police officers.

AN EARLY 1960S PARADE. The Lawrence Police Department heads west on Essex Street. Although pictures of the parades remain, most of them fail to identify the date and reason for the celebration.

HONOR GUARD. Shown here, from left to right, are Officer Sam Incropera, Officer Jerimiah Donovon, Sgt. Clifford Brennan, and, with a broken finger, Officer Alfred Duemling.

THE POLICE MARKSMANSHIP AWARDS CEREMONY IN 1951. Shown here, from left to right, are as follows: (front row) Chief Francis Taynor, Charles F. Hart, Aurthur Flynn (a professional boxer, dressed as a police officer for the part), Lt. Vincent P. Foley, and Ald. of Public Safety William Casey; (middle row) Officer Albert Hashem, Officer Francis McCarthy, Officer Martin Hanley, and Officer Wally Hall; (back row) Officer Charles Vivenzio, Officer Nicholas Trianello, Officer Thomas O'Connor, and Officer John Murphy.

MEDALS AND TROPHIES FOR EVERYONE ON THE SHOOTING TEAM. Receiving the award for the pistol shooting team is Officer Earnest Hart. On the left is Officer Alfred Donovon, and on the right are Alderman of Public Safety Louis Scanlon and Sgt. Charles F. Hart.

THE RETIREMENT OF OFFICER PATRICK FORD ON MAY 22, 1959. Shown here, from left to right, are as follows: (front row) Capt. James Glenn, Officer Francis Landers, Officer Partick Ford, Ald. of Public Safety Louis Scanlon, and Chief Charles F. Hart; (middle row) Officer John Carney, Officer Dennis Danahy, Lt. Everett Dow, Sgt. Francis O'Connor, and Officer Roland Bourget; (back row) Officer Maurice Ferris and Officer Thomas Sabb.

IN THEIR SUNDAY BEST. From left to right, Officer John E. Farrington, Sgt. Joseph Winters, Sgt. Enos Farrington, and Officer John Mulcahy pose for a photograph in their Sunday best.

THE RETIREMENT OF OFFICER LEONARD DUNN IN 1964. Officer Leonard Dunn, wearing a sweater, receives a retirement proclamation from Deputy Chief Daniel Hart, as fellow brother officers look on. The photograph was taken in the Lawrence District Court House at 381 Common Street.

THE RETIREMENT OF GEORGE CONNORS. Shown here, from left to right, are unidentified, Officer Clemment Bennert, Officer George Connors, and Chief Charles F. Hart.

60

SHARING A PROCLAMATION. Shown here, from left to right, are Chief Charles F. Hart, Director of Public Safety Lt. Vincent P. Foley, Officer Francis Landers, Mayor of Lawrence, John J. Buckley, Capt. Frank Fennesey, and Deputy Chief Daniel Hart.

A NEW CONTRACT BEING SIGNED AT CITY HALL. From left to right are as follows: (sitting) Officer Francis Landers, president of the Patrolmans Union; Mayor of Lawrence Daniel Kiley, director of public safety; and Capt. Philip DiAdimo; (standing) Officer William McGuigan, Capt. Carl Schiavone, and an unidentified man.

MAY 1949. Shown here, from left to right, are as follows: (front row) Officer Carl Schiavine, Sgt. Vincent P. Foley, Officer George Connors, Director of Public Safety Louis Scanlon, unidentified, Sgt. Charles F. Hart, Officer Earnest Hart, and Officer Alfred Donovan; (middle row) unidentified, Officer Rollie Bourget, Officer Fred Guilmartin, Officer Thomas O'Connor, Officer Martin Hanley, Officer Francis Landers, and Officer Jerimiah Donovon; (back row) Officer William Ludwig, Officer Gilly Hume, Officer John Concannon, Officer Nicholas Trionello, Officer Daniel Pappa, Officer Jerry Murphy, Officer Francis Incropera Jr., and John Murphy.

LT. FRANCIS INCROPERA JR. WITH THE CITY OF LAWRENCE CROSSING GUARDS. Lieutenant Incropera was in charge of the traffic division at this time.

WILLIAM BARRY. Officer Barry is dressed for a parade in the 1960s.

A 1953 VIEW OF THE BELLEVUE CEMETERY. This police cruiser was already sporting a centennial license plate. In the background, just behind the monument, is the area that 46 years later would become the site of the Lawrence Police Department Memorial. Officers Frank Wieszczcek, standing, and Joseph Mulcahy, inside the car, pose for the camera.

LATE IN THE 1980s. The mayor of Lawrence, Kevin Sullivan, is flanked by the Lawrence Police Honor Guard. Shown here, from left to right, are Sgt. Samuel Coco, Officer Willy Arlqueeuw, Mayor Sullivan, Officer Thomas Murphy, and Sgt. Alfred Petralia, who would later attain the rank of lieutenant.

AN ANNUAL MEETING OF THE POLICE RELIEF ASSOCIATION IN THE 1950s. Shown here, from left to right, are as follows: (front row) Chief Guillman, from Methuen; John J Burke, the district attorney for Essex County; unidentified; Mayor John J. Buckley of Lawrence; retired Chief Charles Vose from Lawrence; unidentified; Ald. of Public Safety Vincent P. Foley; Chief Charles F. Hart from Lawrence; and unidentified; (back row) Officer Francis Landers, president of the Police Relief Association; Deputy Chief of Lawrence Arthur Riley; Judge John Fenton; State Representative Thomas Lane; unidentified; Judge Darcey of the Lawrence District Court; FBI Officer J. Brennan; FBI Officer Donald Scott; North Andover Chief of Police Joseph Lawlor; Andover Chief of Police Dave Nicoll; an unidentified state police officer; and Registry of Motor Vehicles Inspector Ruel.

A LAWRENCE POLICE RELIEF ASSOCIATION
ANNUAL MEETING. Standing in the rear row
are Officer Edward Lawlor; Lt. Vincent P.
Foley, president of the Police Relief
Association; Officer Francis Landers;
Massachusetts State Police Officer Carl
Knightly; and Chief Charles F. Hart. Seated in
the center is retired chief Charles Vose.

THE LAWRENCE POLICE RELIEF ASSOCIATION
AT THE TURN OF THE CENTURY. Officers of
the Lawrence Police Relief Association shown
here, from left to right, are John D. Mahoney,
president; Matthew A. McDonald, vice
president; Sgt. W.G. Spranger, secretary;
Joseph Brooks, Michael J. Moynihan, and
William H. Ahearn, board of directors; and
Joseph Kline, treasurer.

ANNUAL MEETINGS OF THE LAWRENCE POLICE RELIEF ASSOCIATION. Shown in the above photograph, from left to right, are as follows: (front row) unidentified, Judge Fenton, unidentified, unidentified, Mayor John J. Buckley, retired chief Charles Vose, unidentified, unidentified, and Director of Public Safety Vincent P. Foley; (back row) unidentified, unidentified, Officer Joseph Peruse, Capt. James Glenn, Chief Charles F. Hart, Association President Francis Landers, unidentified, Deputy Chief Arthur Riley, unidentified, Chief of Andover David Nicoll, and Registry of Motor Vehicle Inspector Ruel. In the photograph below, from left to right, are the following: (front row) Mayor John J. Buckley on the far left, unidentified, retired chief Charles Vose, Deputy Chief Arthur Riley, unidentified, Police Relief Association President Francis R. Landers, Chief Charles F. Hart, and John J. Burke District Attorney; (back row) unidentified, Capt. Philip DiAdimo, Judge John J. Fenton, Andover Police Chief David Nicoll, and Director of Public Safety Vincent P. Foley.

THE LAWRENCE POLICE DEPARTMENT SOFTBALL TEAM, 1948. Sports played an important role within the Lawrence Police Department. The sporting caps were donated by the *Lawrence Eagle Tribune*. This team photograph was taken at Sullivan Park on Water Street. Sullivan Park was located at what is now the Lawrence Boy and Girls Club. Shown here, from left to right, are as follows: (front row) unidentified, unidentified, Officer Roland Bourget, Lt. Vincent P. Foley, Officer Daniel Lannon, Officer Frank McCarty, unidentified, and Officer Marty Hanley; (back row) Officer Arthur Riley, unidentified, Officer Morris Ferris, Capt. Andrew Griffin, Officer Jerimiah Donovon, unidentified, Louis Scanlon, Lt. Joseph O'Connor, unidentified, Lt. Alfred Donovan, and unidentified.

SPORTS, TEAMWORK, AND GOOD MORALE. Shown here, from left to right, are as follows: (seated) Officer Dennis Murphy; Officer William Jennings; Officer Joseph St. Germain, who would reach the rank of lieutenant and serve as an acting police chief; Officer Daniel Lannon; Joe Simms, owner of local police hangout, Simms Resturant on Lawrence Street, and a sponsor for the police team; and Officer John Danahy; (standing) Officer Anthony Bistany; Officer Joseph DiZoglio; Officer Samuel M. Lopiano, who would rise to the rank of captain; Officer Francis O'Neil; Officer Jerimiah Donovon; and Officer Francis Landers.

AN UNBEATABLE TEAM. Shown here, from left to right, are as follows: (front row) batboy Morris Ferris Jr., Officer Jerimiah Donovon, Officer John Spanks, Officer William Barry, Officer John McCann, Officer Christopher Donovon, Henry Lefrenier, and Coach Bouchard; (back row) Officer William Donovon, Officer Morris Ferris, Officer Daniel Lannon, Officer Martin Hanley, local businessman Ira Nazarian, Officer Roland Bourget, Officer John Murphy, FBI Agent James Brennan, Officer George Andrews, and Officer Frederick Moran. (Courtesy of *Eagle Tribune* Photographer Raymond Maynard.)

OFFICERS FRANCIS LANDERS, SAMUEL M.
LOPIANO, AND VINCENT P. FOLEY IN 1962.

POSING FOR THE CAMERA. Shown here, from left to right, are as follows: (front row) Officer
Robert Blanchette, who rose to the rank of sergeant; Officer Joseph St. Germain; Officer
Martin Blake; Joe Simms; Chief Charles F. Hart; Sam Lopiano; Officer Joseph (Leo) Ouellette,
who would reach the rank of sergeant; and Officer Joseph Dizoglio; (back row) Officer Sam
Incropera; Officer Anthony Bistany; Officer Jerimiah Donovon; Officer Walter Grady, who
later transferred to the North Andover Police Department; William Lees, Sr.; Officer William
Pederick; Officer Michael Riccio; James Brennan; Officer Dennis Murphy; Officer Daniel
Lannon; and Officer John Danahy.

A Police-Sponsored Team on the South Lawrence Common. From left to right are as follows: (front row, dressed in suits) Officer Francis Landers and Director of Public Safety Lt. Vincent P. Foley; (back row, far left) team manager Officer Eugene Scanlon Sr.; (back row, far right) assistant manager Officer Francis O'Neil.

A SMALL LAWRENCE POLICE BALL TEAM. Shown here, from left to right, are as follows: (front row) unidentified, Ira Nazarian, a local business man, Officer Jerimiah Donovon, Officer William Barry, Officer Wally Andrews, and FBI Agent James Brennan; (back row left) Officer William Donovon, Officer Daniel Lannon, and Officer Alfred Duemling; (back row right) Officer Joseph Winters, who would reach the rank of captain and retire as head of detectives.

THE LAWRENCE POLICE ATHLETIC TEAM IN THE 1950S. These members, from left to right, are as follows: (front row) unidentified, Officer Christopher Donovon, Officer John (Taffy) McCann, Officer John Murphy, and Officer Wally Andrews; (back row) unidentified, Officer Daniel Lannon, Officer Jerimiah Donovon, unidentified, and Officer William Donovon. This photograph was taken at the Hayden Scofield Park on Lawrence Street.

PRIOR TO THE BIG GAME. Officer Francis Landers, on the left, poses with Chief of Police Charles F. Hart.

FROM ONE CHIEF TO ANOTHER. Broderick Crawford, a movie star and a chief of a popular television show in the 1950s and 1960s called *The Highway Patrol*, visits Lawrence. Shown here, from left to right, are Chief Charles F. Hart, Broderick Crawford, and Deputy Chief Arthur Riley, who pins an honorary Lawrence Police Badge on the star's chest.

TIME TO MEET THE GOVERNOR OF MASSACHUSETTS. From left to right are Massachusetts State Governor Foster Furcalo, Lt. Robert Bennert, and Chief Charles F. Hart.

BOSTON BRUINS COME TO TOWN. Mr. Wayne Cashman of the Boston Bruins is in the front row, sporting the Boston Bruins blazer. Just behind his left shoulder is Johnny Busyck, also of the Boston Bruins. In the rear row on the left is Officer Daniel Lannon, and all the way to the right is Officer Walter Sliva.

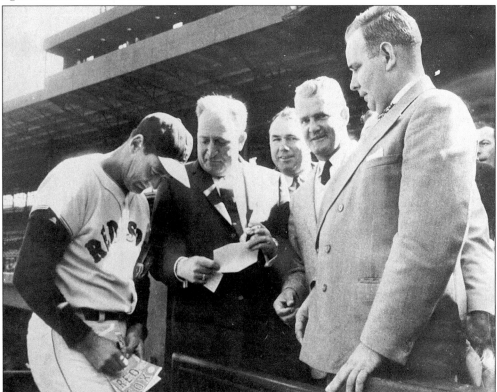

FENWAY PARK, BOSTON, 1957. Shown here, from left to right, are Boston Red Sox player Ted Williams, Officer Frank McCarthy, Officer Jerimiah Donovon, Lt. Vincent P. Foley, and Sgt. Francis Landers.

The Policeman's Ball

Every year, once a year, there was a special event that took place locally, known as the Policeman's Ball. For Lawrence police officers and their wives or girlfriends, it was the social event of the season. It was a time when both superior officers and patrolmen would get together with wives or girlfriends for a formal evening out, complete with dinner and dancing. Trying to get that night off from work to attend was very competitive and went strictly by seniority. No one wanted to miss out.

It started in the 1920s and lasted into the 1970s. Big-name local bands were brought in and a few local politicians made short speeches. Traditionally, it always started the same way: the grand march into the hall led by the police chief and his wife, followed by the superior officers and their dates, then the patrolmen and their wives followed. They saluted to the American Flag, the police chaplain said a short prayer, and dinner was served complete with background music. After dinner, it was dancing and mingling with other guests until midnight.

Dress uniforms for the officers and gowns for the ladies were the uniforms of the day. Many women sported corsages and flowers, given to them by their dates. It was a time for the police department to come together as a family.

THE POLICEMAN'S BALL IN 1971. Shown here, from right to left, are Chief Charles F. Hart with his wife, Celia; Officer William Barry with his wife, Deda; Lt. John Shola with his wife; and the director of public safety, Capt. Philip DiAdimo, with his wife, Marie.

75

CENTRAL CATHOLIC HIGH SCHOOL, 1964. Shown here, from left to right, are Chief Charles F. Hart and his wife, Celia; Officer Francis F. Landers and his wife; Mrs. Buckley and her husband, Mayor of Lawrence John J. Buckley.

PARTICIPANTS IN THE 1968 POLICEMAN'S BALL. Shown here, from left to right, are Chief Charles F. Hart and his wife, Cecilia; an unidentified military officer; Marie DiAdamo and her husband, Director of Public Safety Philip DiAdimo; Ms. Marie Guilmette; and Officer Francis Landers.

COUPLES BOWING THEIR HEADS FOR THE RELIGIOUS INVOCATION PRIOR TO THE START OF
THE POLICEMAN'S BALL IN CENTRAL CATHOLIC HIGH SCHOOL.

POSING FOR THE CAMERA. Shown here, from left to right, are Daniel Kiley, mayor of the City
of Lawrence, with his date in front; Chief Charles F. Hart with wife, Celia in front; Ald. of
Public Safety Vincent P. Foley, with wife, Genevieve; and the president of the Lawrence Police
Relief Association, Officer Francis R. Landers, and his date.

AT THE POLICEMAN'S BALL. From left to right are Chief Daniel P. Kiley and his wife, an unidentified police chaplain, and Mrs. Landers with her husband, Francis R. Landers.

HAMMING IT UP DURING FESTIVITIES. Shown here, from left to right, are Officer William Barry, Officer Frank McCarthy, unidentified, Officer Jerimiah Donovon, unidentified, unidentified, and Officer Christopher Donovon.

Four

ON THE JOB

OFFICER ALFRED PARADIS IN THE LATE 1800S. A copy of this photograph is shown in the Heritage State Park Museum on Jackson Street in Lawrence. (Photograph used with permission of his family.)

OFFICER ALFRED PARADIS AT A CALL BOX IN 1904. This photograph was taken on Valley Street. At that time, the area was heavily populated with French-Canadian people. Officers were assigned to areas that had the same ethnic background as them, so they could act as a liaison for the newcomers and help them settle into their new environments.

THE OFFICE OF THE CHIEF OF POLICE, c. 1920s. Clinton P. Vose sits in his office as the chief of Lawrence Police. The office was in the old station house at the corner of Lawrence Street and Common Street.

CHIEF CHARLES F. HART TAKING CHARGE. Shown here, from left to right, are Officer Thomas J. Sabb and Mr. and Mrs. Senator Edward Kennedy. When the Kennedy's came to town for a political function, Chief Hart took charge of the protection detail himself.

A FINE DISPLAY OF POLICE OFFICERS. Shown here, from left to right, are Officer Marty Hanley, Officer Nicholas Trionello, Capt. Carl Schiavone, Deputy Chief Daniel Hart, Officer George Connors, Chief Daniel Kiley, Lt. Charles F. Hart, and Officer Alfred Donovan.

AN EARLY 1900S PHOTOGRAPH OF THE SQUAD ROOM IN THE STATION HOUSE AT LAWRENCE STREET AND COMMON STREET. These local delegates to the Massachusetts Police Convention are, from left to right, John T. Bradley, unidentified, Officer William Dowe (at the typewriter), Officer Maurice Fitzgerald (far right), and Inspector Fred Lannen (standing).

LOOKING NORTH ON BROADWAY AT THE INTERSECTION OF ESSEX STREET. In the upper left-hand corner of the photograph is a six-sided wooden elevated traffic control box. From this box officers could stay out of the foul weather and direct the flow of traffic using the signals. Its height allowed the officer to see above the traffic to spot any problems.

THE PISTOL-PACKING PRIDE OF NEW ENGLAND. Shown here, from left to right, are Earnest Hart, Sgt. Charles F. Hart, and Officer Daniel Papa. The Lawrence Police Department in the 1950s and 1960s had a shooting team second to none in all of New England. They brought home many awards, medals, and trophies.

NEW ENGLAND POLICE PISTOL TEAM MEDALS OWNED AND WON BY CHARLES F. HART. There are few departments in New England that could match the Lawrence Police Department's skill and number of wins.

PRACTICE MAKES PERFECT. Shown above, from left to right, are Officer John Kobos, the range officer; Methuen Police Officer Warren Archambault in the soft hat and sweater; Lt. Vincent P. Foley with the .45 cal. Thompson sub-machine gun; Officer John (Taffy) McCann with the Winchester 1894 pump shotgun; Officer George Sweeney with the .37 mm. Federal Gas Gun; and an unidentified officer with a .351 cal. Winchester Riot Rifle. In the 1945 photograph below, Lawrence Officer Francis Landers fires the department's .351 cal. Winchester Riot Rifle while Sgt. Francis Incropera Jr. looks on. The range officer behind the barrier is Sgt. Vincent P. Foley.

HONING THEIR SKILLS. Shown here, from left to right, are Officers Daniel Papa, Francis Landers, and Ernest Hart. All are members of the Lawrence Police Shooting Team.

LEFT: LAWRENCE POLICE OFFICER GINO PUGLISI, C. 1950S. *RIGHT:* LT. VINCENT P. FOLEY IN THE 1950S. Foley would later become the Lawrence Director of Public Safety.

LEFT: PATROLMAN VINCENT P. FOLEY. RIGHT: TRAFFIC OFFICER THEODORE (TEDDY) BARDWELL IN THE 1950S.

SGT. ROBERT F. BLACKWELL AND OFFICER WILLIAM A. BARRY IN THE 1960S.

ON THE MOVE, 1960. The man to the left in the photograph above, in the light color soft hat, is Chief Charles F. Hart, who went out on a gaming raid. The officer in the rear in uniform is Daniel Lannon, who later went on to become an expert witness for the State of Massachusetts dealing with gaming cases.

WILLIAM PEDRICK. Officer William Pedrick, in uniform, receives an award from his boss, the alderman of public safety for the City of Lawrence, Lt. Vincent P. Foley.

FRIENDS AND OFFICERS: LT. CLEMENT F. BENNERT
(LEFT) AND CAPT. THOMAS NASTASIA.

OFFICER FRANCIS LANDERS (LEFT) AND OFFICER JAMES
HARVEY POSING FOR A PHOTOGRAPH.

ALDERMAN OF PUBLIC SAFETY ALFRED A. DONOVAN. Donovan was a police captain who successfully ran for alderman of public safety in the 1970s. He also filled in as interim chief of police.

A MEDAL PRESENTATION. Shown here, from left to right, are Lt. Charles F. Hart; Capt. Arthur Riley; Detective Daniel Lannon, who was then a U.S. Navy chief corpsman; and an unidentified officer.

THE RETIREMENT OF LT. VINCENT P. FOLEY IN 1967. Shown here, from left to right, are Officer Edward A. Lawlor, Sgt. Francis Landers, Capt. Samuel M. Lopiano, Lt. Vincent P. Foley (receiving a plaque and a proclamation), Officer Jerimiah Donovon, Chief Charles F. Hart, Director of Public Safety Philip DiAdimo, and Sgt. Frank B. Concemi.

The K-9 Force

The use of dogs in police work came about as a result of the use of dogs during wartime. After the end of World War II, canines proved successful guardians of government property. Many years later officers began to use dogs in police work, and today they form an integral part of policing in modern society.

Many different breeds of dogs have been tried, but the favorite is the German Shepherd for work in both drugs and for attacking. The dogs are sworn police officers and considered a part of the patrol force. They are very loyal to their handlers and a strong bond is most always formed between man and dog. They are more than energetic when it comes time for them to work. We welcome their use within the Lawrence Police Department.

Sent into large buildings to search for someone hiding inside, or to detect for the concealment of drugs, they accomplish in minutes what would take many officers hours of work. In times of gang activity or civil unrest, merely opening the back door to a K-9 cruiser and letting out a snapping, growling 125-pound attack dog dragging its handler on a short leash is enough incentive to disperse large groups of people in a hurry.

Hitting or injuring a working police dog carries the same penalties as hitting a police officer.

K-9 Officer David Augusta Jr. with Agar, His Working Partner.

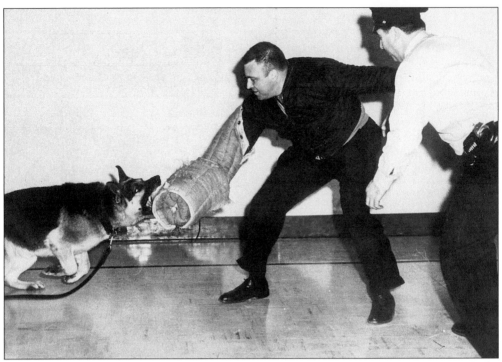

NICE DOGGIE! Hans, the police dog, takes center stage at a demonstration. Helping with the training is Officer Willy Arlequeew with a special sleeve. Hans' handler is Officer Joseph L. DiZoglio on the right.

SGT. ROBERT FARRINGTON WITH MAGNUM, HIS WORKING K-9 PARTNER. K-9 officers take these dogs home and care for them there.

K-9 Officer Michael Padellaro with Xavier, His Working Partner. The dogs are trained not to accept food or treats from anyone other than the dog's trainer. This protects the dogs from being drugged or poisoned. Most often if the K-9 officer leaves the job or is killed, his dog will have to be put down.

On Saint Patrick's Day, even the K-9's are Irish. Shown here, from left to right, are Officer John E. Farrington, Hans, and Officer William McGuigan.

PARTNERS AND FRIENDS. K-9 officer Harry Maldonado takes time out from rigorous training to pose with his K-9 Ruger. Many hours of hard work go into the training of a police dog.

OFFICER SANDRA PICARD AND HER LOYAL WORKING K-9 PARTNER, KAI. Special police cars have to be fitted to accommodate these dogs. The rear seats are removed and replaced with one-piece fiberglass units.

A Much Different View than Schoolchildren Might See Watching a Demonstration by "Officer Friendly" on how Police Dogs Obey Commands. Here Officer David Augusta Sr. puts his K-9 partner, Rocky, through the working course. This is the bad guy's view, only with more restraint by the officer. As you can see, the 100-pound dog is uncomfortably just below the waist level with snapping, growling jaws, just looking for a taste of justice.

THE SWEARING IN OF NEW LAWRENCE POLICE OFFICERS IN 1961 IN LAWRENCE CITY HALL. Shown here, from left to right, are as follows: City Clerk Charles Nyan; Director of Public Safety Vincent P. Foley; (first row) Officers Robert Blanchette and Robert Brown; (second row) Officers Francis O'Neil and Francis Incropera III; (third row) Officers Joseph Dizoglio and John Caveretta; (fourth row) Officers James Harvey and Alfred McGrath.

NEW RECRUITS BEING SWORN IN. Shown here, from left to right, are Ald. of Public Safety Vincent P. Foley, Lawrence City Clerk Joseph Smith, Officer Samuel Nitto, Officer Alfred McGrath (who would later become the assistant clerk of courts for Essex County), and Officer William Pedrick.

THE SWEARING IN CEREMONY FOR NEW LAWRENCE POLICE OFFICERS IN OCTOBER 1988. Standing to the far right in civilian clothes is City Clerk Charles Nyan. Standing to his right in uniform is Capt. Thomas Nastasia. The officers being sworn in, from left to right, are Jose Linares, James Thomas, Kevin Callahan, David Levesque, Paul Plantamura, Michael Padelarro, Emil DeFusco Jr., and Carlos Gonzalas.

NEW RECRUITS IN 1994. Shown here, from left to right, are Officers Michael McCarthy, Michael Navaria, and Thomas Burke.

THE RETIREMENT OF OFFICER GEORGE CONNORS ON SATURDAY SEPTEMBER 28, 1957 IN THE GUARDROOM OF THE LAWRENCE STREET POLICE STATION. Standing in the doorway just under the sign and wearing dark glasses is Officer William McGuigan. Officer George Connors stands on the podium and is presented with a radio from Deputy Chief Daniel Hart. To the deputy chief's left are Officers Charles Vivenzio and Lionel Dube.

RETIREMENT DAY ON EASTER SUNDAY, 1954. Capt. John Casey takes a last look at his tools of the trade before he surrenders them to the chief at his retirement. Capt. Casey appears on p. 34 in the 1920s as a young officer riding in the mounted unit.

NEW RECRUITS LOOKING READY FOR ACTION. Shown here, from left to right, are Officer Samual Coco, Officer William Hale Sr., Officer Joseph Girgenti, Officer John Spaziano, Officer Terrance Schiavone, and Capt. Carl Schiavone.

OFFICERS ON GRADUATION DAY FROM THE SOMMERVILLE MASSACHUSETTS POLICE ACADEMY, MAY 19, 1989. Shown here, from left to right, are Officers Sean Burke, Stephen O'Connor (who later became a Massachusetts State police officer), Kevin Callahan (class valedictorian), Albert Inostroza, and James Thomas.

TWO OFFICERS RETIRING FROM THE LAWRENCE POLICE DEPARTMENT, 1955. The two retiring officers are in suits in the center of the front row, holding the radios they received as gifts from the department. Of the officers shown here, only Gino Paglisi, fourth from the right, has been identified.

AN AWARD PRESENTATION IN THE GUARDROOM OF THE 90 LOWELL STREET STATION. Shown here, from left to right, are as follows: (first row) Capt. Thomas Nastasia, Officer Kenneth Wall, Officer William Barry, Officer Eugen Scanlon, and Officer Edmond Daher; (middle row) Capt. Steven Sciuto Jr., Officer Thomas Carroll, Officer John Concannon, and Samual Coco. Receiving congratulations is William Jennings. Giving him the award is Ald. of Public Safety Philip DiAdimo. Behind them are Officer Gilly Hume and Chief Charles F. Hart.

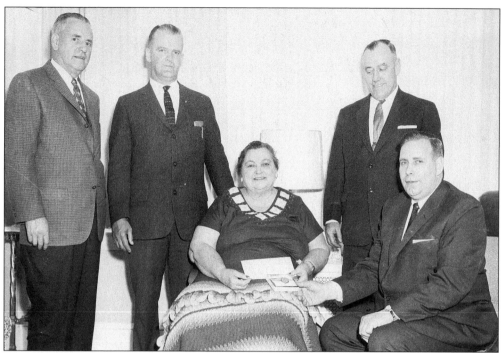

THE RETIREMENT OF INSPECTOR BEATRICE CLARKE ON JUNE 1, 1960. Her name shows up on many arrest reports in the span of her career as an inspector assigned to the vice unit. From left to right are Lt. Robert Bennert, Director of Public Safety Vincent P. Foley, Officer Beatrice Clarke, Chief Charles F. Hart, and Officer Francis Landers, president of the Patrolman's Union.

THE LINEUP. Shown here, from left to right, are as follows: (front row) Officer Walter Sliva, Officer Francis R. Landers, Ald. Vincent P. Foley, Chief Charles F. Hart, and Officer Francis McCarthy; (back row) Officer William P. McGuigan, Officer Roland Bourget, and Officer Jerimiah Donovon.

CAPTAIN MCCORMICK, 1957. Shown here, from left to right, are Sgt. Alfred Donovan, Officer Francis Landers, Captain McCormick, Lt. Fennesey, and Lt. Philip DiAdimo.

RUNNING FOR ELECTION. Many officers from within the Lawrence Police Department ran for local public office. Some were successful while others were not. The most coveted position was director of public safety.

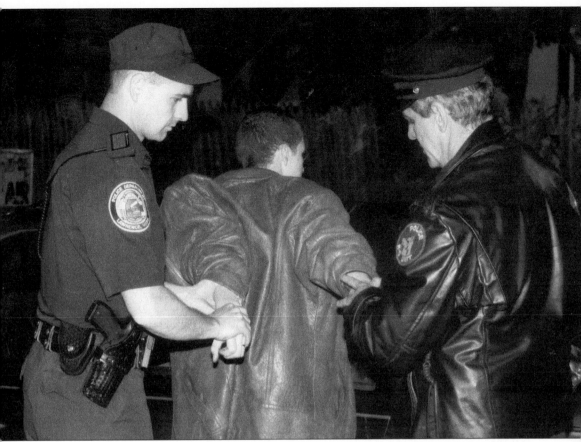

FATHER AND SON MAKE THE ARREST. Officer David Augusta Jr. (left) and Officer David Augusta Sr. handcuff a criminal suspect. They were not partners this night, but responded to the same call and soon had the problem well in hand.

FATHER AND TWO SONS: THREE FAMILY MEMBERS OF THE LAWRENCE POLICE DEPARTMENT.
From left to right are Capt. Carl Schiavone, Officer and Alderman of Public Safety Terrance Schiavone, and Chief of Police Patrick Schiavone.

FATHER AND SON.
Thomas Carroll Jr. (left) is shown here with his dad, Officer Thomas Carroll Sr., on duty outside Central Catholic High School.

HUSBAND AND WIFE. On the left is Officer Dawn Pappalardo with her arm around her husband, Officer Paul Plantamura. They are both patrol officers on the day shift, but do not ride together.

SGT. EMIL DEFUSCO SR. (LEFT) AND EMIL DEFUSCO, JR (RIGHT). The father works the midnight shift while the son works patrol on days.

DIRECTING TRAFFIC. Officer John J. Spanks gives directions while directing the flow of traffic from his traffic box at the intersection of Essex Street and Lawrence Street.

OFFICER JOHN J. SPANKS IN HIS DRESS UNIFORM IN THE EARLY 1950S.

OFFICER STEPHEN J. FERRIS SR. POSING IN 1929.

IN THE EARLY 1950s. Neither rain, sleet, or snow stopped John J. Spanks from keeping the traffic flowing smoothly.

OFFICER GINO PUGLISI STANDING
TRAFFIC DUTY IN FRONT OF THE
LAWRENCE STREET CONGREGATIONAL
CHURCH AT THE CORNER OF
LAWRENCE STREET AND HAVERHILL
STREET.

OFFICER GINO PUGLISI AT HIS USUAL
TRAFFIC ASSIGNMENT AT THE
INTERSECTION OF LAWRENCE STREET
AND HAVERHILL STREET. Officer
Puglisi was responsible for the safety of
students crossing the street after exiting
Lawrence High School. Many of the
students remember him fondly.

**OFFICER JOHN J. SPANKS DIRECTING
TRAFFIC ON ESSEX STREET AT THE
INTERSECTION OF AMESBURY STREET.**
Officer Spanks is facing west on Essex
Street.

THE HAZARDS OF RIDING DOUBLE, C. 1950S. As if posing for a Norman Rockwell painting,
Lt. Francis Incropera Jr. gives two young boys advice about the hazards of riding double.

OFFICER WILLY ARLEQUEEW AND OFFICER FRANK FOLEY, READY FOR ACTION, C. 1960S. Officer Frank Foley went on to become a captain in the Lawrence Police Department.

SHOWING OFF THE NEW POLICE CRUISERS. From left to right are Chief of Detectives Capt. Joseph Fitzpatrick, Mayor of Lawrence Kevin Sullivan, and Lt. Gregory Panagiotakos.

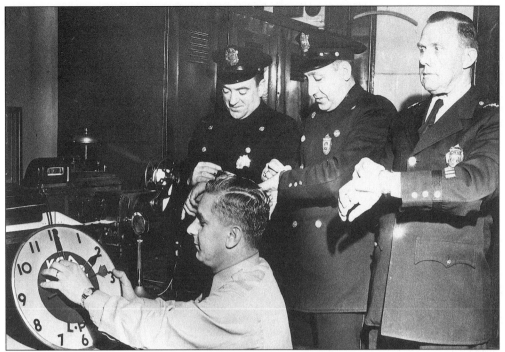

CHANGING TO DAYLIGHT SAVINGS TIME, APRIL 25, 1958. Shown here, from left to right, are as follows: (standing) Officer Joseph Winters, Officer Aurthur Gillis, and Deputy Chief Capt. Daniel Hart; (sitting) Daniel Lovallo. This photograph was taken in the communications room at the Lawrence Street police station.

CHECKING OUT A NICE RECOVERY OF STOLEN PROPERTY. From left to right are Officer Daniel Lannon, Capt. Francis Fennesey, and Officer Michael Murphy.

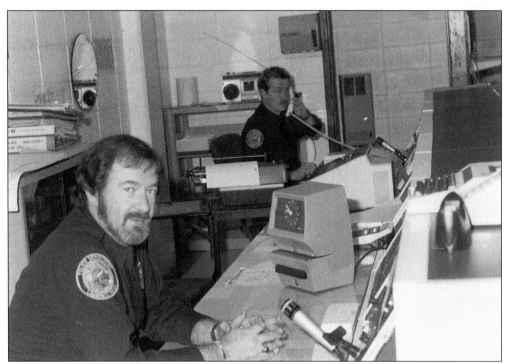

MODERN COMMUNICATIONS FOR THE DEPARTMENT IN THE EARLY 1990S. Seated in the telecommunications room are Officer Edgar St. Onge (left) and Officer Jeffrey Lannon. At the time, calls were received, written down on cards, and walked into the communications room, where they were received, stamped with the time and date, and dispatched out by radio.

LOOKING SOUTH DOWN BROADWAY. An unidentified Lawrence police officer directs traffic at the intersection of Haverhill Street and Broadway.

AN UNIDENTIFIED LAWRENCE POLICE OFFICER DIRECTING TRAFFIC AT THE INTERSECTION OF HAVERHILL STREET AND BROADWAY. The only thing missing is the traffic. We are looking north up Broadway.

ACCEPTING AN AWARD. From left to right are Traffic Officer William Barry, Lt. Philip DiAdimo, Capt. Andy Griffen, unidentified, and Sgt. Francis Landers.

OFFICERS WILLY ARLEQUEEW AND OFFICER JOSEPH (LEO) OUELLETTE INVESTIGATING A FATAL ACCIDENT. A man was killed when a cable holding a paint scaffolding parted; the man plunged to the ground.

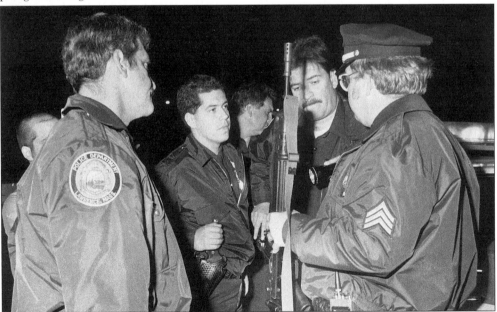

ANOTHER SEMI-AUTOMATIC WEAPON BEING TAKEN OFF OF THE STREETS. Shown here, from left to right, are Officer David Augusta Sr., Officer Jose Martinez, Officer John Reily (who is partially hidden in the rear), Officer James Houlihan, and Sgt. Calvin Hall. (Photographed by Mr. Carl Russo.)

ABOVE AND BEYOND THE CALL OF DUTY. Shown here, from left to right, are as follows: (front row) Sgt. Samuel Coco; Detective Anthony Vallante; Detective Gene Hatem, who became sergeant; and Detective and Officer Michael Callihan in the blonde female wig; (back row) Detective Brian Burokas, looking over Officer Callahan's shoulder; Sgt. Detective Alfred Petralia, who became lieutenant; and Officer Michael Molchan, who became captain of detectives. Officer Michael Callahan was dressed as a female and sent out into the street as a female decoy prostitute. Believe it or not, it resulted in many arrests.

A NIGHT SHIFT PARTY TO CELEBRATE SGT. DANIEL FOLEY'S PROMOTION TO ACTING LIEUTENANT. Shown here, from left to right, are as follows: (kneeling) Officer Richard Brooks, Officer Michael Carelli, and Officer Justin Hart; (standing) Sgt. Raymond Smith, Officer Ronald J. DeSantis, Officer Sean Burke, Officer Mary Bartlett, Officer Arthur Waller, Officer Carlos Gonzalas, Officer Michael McCarthy, Lt. Daniel P. Foley, Sgt. Robert Blanchette (in the dark glasses), Officer Emil DeFuso Jr., Officer William Beck, Officer Paul Karamourtopoulos, Officer Alan Andrews, Officer Frank Giarrusso, Sgt. Stephen Tarkesian, and Officer Anthony Vallente.

BEST OF FRIENDS. Officer Thomas Carroll (left) poses with Sgt. Robert Blackwell.

GOOD FRIENDS AND FELLOW OFFICERS. Shown here are Officers Willy Arlequeew (standing) and James Toomey.

BEST FRIENDS SHARE THE POLICEMAN OF THE YEAR AWARD IN 1989. Officer Gene Hatem (left) and Officer Anthony Vallante accept the 1989 award. Officer Vallante would later transfer to the Andover Massachusetts Police Department.

A GOOD HAUL IN ANY TIME PERIOD, AUGUST 26, 1997. Under the direction of Detective Lt. Alfred Petralia, standing in plain clothes, Motor Officer Kevin Callahan (right) and Officer David Lavesque (left) show the haul of drugs and money recovered in a raid. They recovered over $8,000 dollars in cash and 350 grams of heroin from Lawrence streets.

A Preserved Piece of the Past. This yellow brick was taken from the old police station at the corner of Lawrence Street and Common Street when it was torn down. It was made into a plaque and presented to Capt. Joseph Fitzpatrick when he was made captain in 1977.

Officer Ronald J. DeSantis Demonstrating the Use of the Police Call Box that Was Used into the 1970s.

OFFICER DOMENIC ARMANO IN A THREE-WHEELED CUSHMAN TRAFFIC VEHICLE USED IN THE DOWNTOWN AREA FOR TRAFFIC ENFORCEMENT IN THE 1970S AND 1980S. Officer Armano retired and now serves on the Lawrence City Council.

Killed in the Line of Duty

When this message comes across the tele-type screen, no matter where it is sent from, it strikes sadness in the hearts of all police officers everywhere. The grim message has no geographical boundary for us. We know in our hearts it could have been any one of us, whose name could have come across on that tele-type. We know that some police officer somewhere never went home after his tour of duty was over. Some mother, wife, husband, or child will be crying tonight, with a broken heart for those officers that laid down their lives for mankind. The message, no matter what it officially says, means that part of us as police officers, and part of all of us as Americans, has died.

In our 152-year history in Lawrence, Massachusetts, we have only had to send that message out over the wire twice. One message was sent out for Officer Peter J. Manning in 1953 and then again in 1990 for Officer Thomas J. Duggan Sr. We hope that we as a department never again have to send out a message that one of our police officers has been killed in the line of duty.

THE FINAL MARCH FOR OFFICER THOMAS J. DUGGAN IN 1990. And so it begins—the formation of the final march that will lead slain officer Thomas J. Duggan to his final resting-place. Represented in the formation were many outside federal, state, and county agencies. Honor Guard leader David Augusta Sr. puts the officers in formation and sets the pace for the march.

CHIEF ALLAN COLE MARCHING OUT FRONT ALONE. Chief Allan Cole leads his men in formation west up Manchester Street toward the cemetery.

SILENT MOURNERS. A solemn, sad-faced police department walks silently to Saint Mary's cemetery to lay brother officer Thomas J. Duggan to rest. The procession stretched out over 2 miles. There was not a man with a dry eye.

A GRIM PASSING. The United States Flag passed to Officer Duggan's friend, Officer Robert Grant Jr., was then passed to the grieving widow, Pamela Duggan, and her family.

IN MEMORIAM. The retired badge, #80, and a box key belonging to Thomas J. Duggan hangs on this plaque in the lobby of the Lawrence Police Station.

122

A Photograph of Officer Thomas J. Duggan Jr. Hanging inside the Lobby of the Police Station with Some of the Citizens of Lawrence that He Faithfully Served and Died Protecting.

The Police Memorial in Miami, Florida, where Officer Thomas Duggan's Name Appears.

AUX. OFF. AUBREY WILLIAMS, NORTH OLMSTED, OH

MER, AL   CPL. HARRY L. KINIKIN, JR., PRINCE GEC

A STATE PATROL   AGENT DOUGLAS ABRAM, F.B.I. DC

GREENEY, III, BROWARD CO., FL   RNGR. CLAYTON (

C   PTL. THOMAS J. DUGGAN, LAWRENCE, MA   CH

E POLICE   DET. SGT. GARY D. WILSON, DULUTH, M

TRPR. MERLE E. DEWITT, CA HWY. PATROL

THE WALL OF REMEMBRANCE AT THE POLICE MEMORIAL IN MIAMI, FLORIDA. The name of Officer Duggan can be seen as it is on the memorial.

The Lawrence Police Memorial

The City of Lawrence Police Memorial was dedicated on October 18, 1997, at noon. The dedication was attended by over 500 people, both civilians and police. The memorial began as an idea in late July 1997, to do something special for the police department's 150th anniversary. In just those few short months, a committee of eight police officers managed, with much hard work and perseverance, to build this spectacular monument to all Lawrence police officers. It stands today in the Bellevue Cemetery as a monument built with pride.

The committee was made up of the following men: President Officer Ronald J. DeSantis; Vice President Officer Shawn Conway; and committee members Officer Michael McGrath, Officer Richard O'Connell, Officer Justin Hart, Officer Jose Flores Jr., Officer Michael McCarthy, and Officer Roy Vasque. The memorial was built at a cost of about $5,000. There was a lot of help from many individuals who donated their time, effort, and energy to the project. Granite paving stones were sold at a cost of $75 each to help raise funds for the project. Those bricks were placed into a walkway, Heroes Walk, that lead to the main monument. The bricks included the names of officers, past and present. Room was left for expansion of the walkway for many years to come. There is a main monument that weighs in at 3,500 pounds, and two smaller monuments for the two officers killed in the line of duty, Officers Thomas J. Duggan and Peter Manning. The wording on the main monument was written by Officer Ronald J. DeSantis and reads: Dedicated to all police officers, past, present and future who faithfully serve the citizens of Lawrence, Massachusetts.

The monument is surrounded by five flagpoles. The tallest, directly behind the main monument, is 25 feet tall and flies the United States Flag. The first United States Flag to be raised on the site was the one from the coffin of Officer Duggan. The other flagpoles are 20 feet tall and fly the Massachusetts State Flag, the City of Lawrence Flag, the Lawrence Police Department Flag, and the Prisoners of War Flag. The two streets directly surrounding the memorial were renamed for Officer Duggan and Officer Manning, and were marked with two granite street signs.

FINISHED AND DEDICATED. This was beginning of a life for a police memorial.

DEDICATION DAY, OCTOBER 18, 1997. The flag from the coffin of slain officer Thomas J. Duggan is raised to the top of the flag pole by Officer David Augusta Sr., head of the Lawrence Police Color Guard.

WORK BEGINNING AT THE FUTURE SITE OF THE POLICE MEMORIAL. Standing with a shovel on the left is Chief Robert E. Hayden Jr.; on the right is the president of the committee, Officer Ronald J. DeSantis. The others, from left to right, are as follows: (kneeling committee members) Officers Justin Hart, Richard O'Connell, and Michael McGrath; (standing) the vice president, Officer Shawn Conway, Officer Jose Flores Jr., Michael McCarthy, and Officer Roy Vasque.

126

AN ARTIST'S CONCEPTION. From this the finished product the monument grew into reality.

WALKWAY CONSTRUCTION BEGINS. Union Masons Butch and Richard Foggarty unselfishly donated their time, effort, and energy. We thank them for it. Here they lay out Hero's Walk, paved with the names of Lawrence police officers.

THE COMMITTEE MARKER PLACED AT THE VERY TOP OF HERO'S WALK. It lists the committee members who worked so hard to accomplish this monument.

THE MAIN STONE. The main stone is 8 feet by 4 feet by 10 inches thick and weighs approximately 3,800 pounds.